This book belongs to:

_____

Name

_____

Phone Number

_____

Date

Bible Study Coach:

_____

Name

_____

Phone Number

DISCOVER
GOD'S EXCHANGE
THE GOSPEL FOR YOUTH

JEFF MUSGRAVE WITH TINA PARRY

Discover God's Exchange: The Gospel for Youth
© 2022 Jeff Musgrave

ISBN: 978 1 94429 892 0

Cover Design by Justin Hall
Interior Design by Niddy Griddy Design, Inc.
Illustrations by Manny Juah
Dedication Portrait Illustration by Jisu Jekel Art
Coach's Supplement written by Karen Pickering

Printed in the United States of America
1 2 3 4 5 6 7 8 Printing/Year 25 24 23 22

Evelyn Mitchell loved children and children loved her. For many years she taught children's Sunday School classes and helped with a Bible memory program for youth. If you were to walk into her kitchen on a Saturday afternoon, you would have found her cutting out flannelgraph characters and diligently preparing her Sunday School lesson. The day she finally retired from teaching was a sad day for the young people and parents of her church. A children's song was on her lips the day she left this earth for heaven: "Let it shine! Let it shine! Let it shine!"

This book was made possible through generous gifts from her family and friends.

CONTENTS

INTRODUCTION

You've probably heard a lot of people mention God in daily life—phrases like "God bless you," "God, help us," or "God loves you!" We even speak of God every time we say the Pledge of Allegiance! Can you think of that phrase in the pledge?

One nation u_____ G_____, indivisible, with liberty and justice for all.

We hear people talk about God, but many people do not actually know who God is! That's what this study is all about—teaching you who God is, what He's done for YOU, and what He wants for YOUR life. Just think—after finishing this study, you'll know more about God than many adults do! More importantly, you'll be able to have a close relationship with God.

As you work through this Bible study, it is best if you meet with a Bible coach after completing each lesson to discuss what you are learning. Even though we have included the Scripture verses in this book, you may want to have your Bible handy to underline verses that you want to especially remember. If you feel that you need help as you go through each lesson, you can choose to work with your coach to study the lessons.

If you stick with it, this study will teach you truths about God that could change your life! When you finish, there is a certificate at the end of the study to reward your hard work.

OK, are you ready? Let's get started with Lesson 1!

LESSON 1
GOD IS HOLY

LESSON 1
GOD IS HOLY

Have you ever read a biography or autobiography of someone's life? If so, who did you read about? _____ When you read biographies, you learn where people were born, where they lived, what kind of people they were, etc. In many ways, the Bible is like a biography. It is a book written by God that tells us who He is. He wants you to know about Him so you can be close to Him. This study will show you four important things the Bible says about God:

God is holy.
God is just.
God is loving.
God is full of grace.

Let's start by learning how the Bible was written so you know that what it says is true.

1. Read the Bible verse below that tells us how the Bible was written, and then check the box for each correct answer.

> **All Scripture [the Bible] is breathed out by God and profitable for teaching, for reproof, for correction, and for training in righteousness. ~2 Timothy 3:16**

Who breathed out the Bible?

☐ **People**   ☐ **Animals**   ☐ **God**

How much of the Bible was spoken or "breathed out" by God?

☐ **All of the Bible**   ☐ **Some of the Bible**   ☐ **Most of the Bible**

The Bible came to us from the mouth of God, so we can trust that everything it says is true. So, let's get started in the place you normally start in a book—at the very beginning! If you have a Bible, you can try finding this verse for yourself—Genesis 1:1.

Were you able to find it in your Bible?

☐ Yes!   ☐ No!

If you weren't able to find it, in your next meeting with your Bible coach, ask how to find verses in the Bible. It's kind of like understanding a secret code!

2. Read the Bible verse below.

> **In the beginning, God created the heavens and the earth.**
> **~Genesis 1:1**

Who made the world and created life?

☐ **Monkeys**   ☐ **Adam**   ☐ **God**   ☐ **An explosion in space**

You will hear a lot of different ideas about how the world began, but the Bible is very clear that in the beginning of time God created the world and everything in it. That means He created YOU! Let's find out more about the God who made you! This lesson will cover one of the most important facts or qualities about God—He is holy.

3. Read the verse below that tells us what this quality is.

> **Holy, holy, holy, is the Lord God Almighty, who was and is and is to come! ~Revelation 4:8**

This verse tells us that God is h_____.

4. Which of these words do you think means the same as holy?

☐ **Kind**   ☐ **Rich**   ☐ **Perfect**   ☐ **Big**

Probably the place most people have seen the word *holy* is on the cover of a Bible—Holy Bible. The word *holy* means "perfect or sinless." God is holy—He has never sinned or done anything wrong!

5. Read this awesome verse about God!

> **There is none holy like the LORD: for there is none besides you. ~1 Samuel 2:2**

Who does the Bible say is holy like God is holy?

☐ **None**   ☐ **A few**   ☐ **Some**   ☐ **Most**

Yes, the Bible says that only God is holy or perfect. He always does what is right, and He has never done anything wrong. Have you ever done anything wrong? You may think . . . "Well, how do you know what's right and wrong? Who decides if something is right or wrong? My parents? My teachers? Me?"

That's a good question! Since God made the world and everything in it, He made the rules we all should follow. Have you ever heard of the Ten

Commandments? They are ten basic laws in the Bible that help us know what God says is right and wrong (see Exodus 20).

Most of God's laws start with the words "You shall not . . ." Let's look at a few of them to help you figure out if you've ever broken any of God's laws.

God's Law

6. One of the Ten Commandments is "Honor your father and mother."

| **Honor your father and your mother, that your days may be long in the land that the Lord your God is giving you. ~Exodus 20:12**

God wants you to obey and respect your f_____ and m_____ all the time—immediately, completely, and with a good attitude.

How often would you say you obey (honor) and respect your parents when they tell you to do something?

☐ **Every single time**   ☐ **Most of the time**   ☐ **Not very often**
☐ **Never**

Let's be honest, we can never say that we've obeyed and honored our parents every single time!

7. So, have you ever broken God's law of obeying and honoring your parents?

☐ **Yes**   ☐ **No**

Are you holy and perfect like God?

☐ **Yes**   ☐ **No**

8. Another law God gave us is "Don't lie."

> **You shall not bear false witness [lie] against your neighbor.**
> **~Exodus 20:16**

God tells us that we should never tell a l_____.

Have you ever lied to someone before?

☐ **Yes**   ☐ **No**

Are you holy and perfect like God?

☐ **Yes**   ☐ **No**

9. Another law God gave us is "Don't steal."

> **You shall not steal. ~Exodus 20:15**

God tells us we should never s_____ something that belongs to someone else.

Have you ever taken something that was not yours?

☐ Yes   ☐ No

Are you holy and perfect like God?

☐ Yes   ☐ No

If you want to, you can look up more of the commandments. You can find them in Exodus 20:1-17 in your own Bible. Write down some of the other commandments God gave us!

But God's laws are more than just rules to live by. They help us understand what God is like.

10. For example, what does God's command not to lie tell us about God?

God is t_____.

The reason God tells us not to lie is because He is truth. Every time we lie, we offend God. That hurts our relationship with Him. God made us to have a close relationship with Him. When we're not close to God, we often feel sad.

Have you ever felt guilty or lonely or empty inside?

☐ Yes   ☐ No

God wants you to be close to Him! Then you can feel peaceful in your heart.

OUR PROBLEM

11. This leaves us with a problem because the Bible says we have all sinned.

| All have sinned and fall short of the glory of God. ~Romans 3:23

How many people have sinned and broken God's law?

☐ All   ☐ Most   ☐ Some   ☐ A few

19

This verse also tells us that we have fallen s_____ of God's glory.

So, the Bible says all of us have sinned and fall short of God's glory. What does that mean? Think of it this way. Imagine looking at the top of a flagpole and someone saying, "Hey, jump and touch the top of that flagpole!" Let's say that you try your best and jump as high as you can.

Did you reach the top?

☐ Yes   ☐ No

No! There's no way you could reach the top!

Now let's say that you told an Olympic high jump gold medalist to jump to the top of the flagpole.
Would he get closer to the top than you did?

☐ Yes   ☐ No

Of course, he would jump higher than you, but would even he be able to touch the top of the flagpole?

☐ Yes   ☐ No

Even though the Olympian would jump higher and get closer to the top of the flagpole, he would still "fall short" of the goal. That's how it is with trying to be perfect like God. You may do more good things than others, but all of us sin. All of us "fall short of the glory of God."

Most people realize they are sinners and are not perfect like God. What many may not understand is that our sin keeps us from having a close relationship with our holy God.

12. What do you think it takes to have a relationship with God and live together with Him in heaven?_____

_____

_____

13. Are you 100 percent sure that your sins are forgiven and that you're going to heaven?

☐ Yes   ☐ No   ☐ Maybe

Ending Thoughts

14. What did you learn about God and about yourself today?

God is ☐ sinful ☐ holy

I am ☐ sinful ☐ holy

Right, you've learned that we are all sinful and God is holy. If you stopped studying about God and yourself right now, it would be pretty discouraging! Meet with your Bible coach and start the next lesson to learn more about God. I promise, this study ends with Good News! If you don't want to wait to find out, feel free to ask your Bible coach to show you from the Bible how your sins can be forgiven.

If you have any questions about this lesson that you want to ask your Bible coach, write them here:

_____

_____

_____

_____

_____

_____

_____

Congratulations on finishing the first lesson! You're doing great!

Will you promise to finish the next lesson, too?

☐ Yes ☐ No

LESSON 2
GOD IS JUST

LESSON 2
GOD IS JUST

In Lesson 1, we learned that God is holy. We also learned that because we are sinners, it's impossible to have a relationship with a holy God and go to heaven! This lesson focuses on another quality of God—that He is just. What does that mean?

Even if you haven't ever heard someone described as "just," you've probably heard the word *justice*. You recite it in the Pledge of Allegiance: "with liberty and justice for all." You may have heard someone say they "demand justice" when a person wrongs them. *Justice* means getting the reward or the punishment that a person deserves for his actions. When we say that God is just, it means that He cannot ignore our sin. He has to punish sin since He is the perfect Judge.

1. Here are some verses that tell us that God is just. (Circle) the word *just* or *justice* in each verse.

> The Rock, his work is perfect, for all his ways are justice. A God of faithfulness and without iniquity, just and upright is he. ~Deuteronomy 32:4

> The works of his hands are faithful and just. ~Psalm 111:7

> The LORD . . . is righteous; he does no injustice; every morning he shows forth his justice; each dawn he does not fail. ~Zephaniah 3:5

If God were to ignore or overlook your sin, would He be a *just* God?

☐ Yes   ☐ No

THE PUNISHMENT FOR SIN

2. Since God is just, He has to punish sin. Let's look at what the punishment for sin is.

> For the wages [payment] of sin is death. ~Romans 6:23

What does this verse say is the payment or punishment for sin? D_____

This death is in a place often called hell. Some people believe hell is an imaginary place, not a real place. But when Jesus lived on earth, He taught more about hell than heaven. Does God want people to go to hell? No! He tells us about hell because He doesn't want us to go there. Here are some verses that make it clear that God will judge us and that hell is a real place:

> It is appointed for man to die once, and after that comes judgment. ~Hebrews 9:27

> Then he will say to those on his left, "Depart from me, you cursed, into the eternal fire prepared for the devil and his angels." ~Matthew 25:41

> These will go away into eternal punishment, but the righteous into eternal life. ~Matthew 25:46

3. This verse is very clear about who will go to hell (the lake of fire).

> But as for the cowardly, the faithless, the detestable, as for murderers, the sexually immoral, sorcerers, idolaters, and all liars, their portion will be in the lake that burns with fire and sulfur, which is the second death. ~Revelation 21:8

According to this verse, who will be in this lake of fire? All l_____

This is a rough list and maybe you're thinking you haven't done most of those things, but have you ever told a lie?

☐ Yes   ☐ No

If you think, *But that doesn't make me a liar*, think about this: How many murders do you have to commit to be a murderer?

☐ One   ☐ Several

Yes, it only takes one murder to be a murderer! So, how many lies do you have to tell to be a liar?

☐ One   ☐ Several

The truth is, we've all told many more lies than just one, which makes us all liars and deserving of death in hell.

THE NEED FOR JUSTICE

You might say, "But I thought God was a loving God! How can He judge people and send them to an awful place like hell?" Here's an illustration that might help you understand how important it is for a loving God to be just and to punish sin.

4. Imagine a judge in your town who was in charge of deciding the punishment for a man who killed your friend.

Would the judge be a good, just judge if he overlooked that man's crime of murder?

☐ Yes   ☐ No

Why or why not? _____

_____

_____

_____

_____

What if the judge said, "But I love this murderer! He is my brother. I love him too much to punish his crime of murder!"

Would he now be a good judge to overlook his brother's crime?

☐ Yes   ☐ No

Why or why not? _____

_____

_____

_____

_____

Even though the judge loved the murderer, it is still not just and right to allow this crime to go unpunished. In the same way, God cannot tolerate our sin or pretend it didn't happen. He is holy and just, and our sin must be punished.

ENDING THOUGHTS

5. Based on what you've learned from the Bible so far, if you were to die right now, where would you go? _____

Why? _____

_____

_____

_____

_____

You may still be wondering, "So, how does God show His love to me if He has to punish my sin?" Good question! That prepares us for our next lesson, which shows us that God is loving! He loves you so much that He provided a way for you to be close to Him. That is the Good News that *Discover God's Exchange* was written to tell you about!

_____, God does not want you to go to hell!
(write your name)

> **For I have no pleasure in the death of anyone, declares the Lord God; so turn, and live. ~Ezekiel 18:32**

What does this verse say He wants you to do right now? T_____
and l_____!

Lessons 3 and 4 will teach you how to *turn* from your sins and *live.* If you don't want to wait to find out how, feel free to ask your Bible coach to show you from the Bible how your sins can be forgiven.

If you have any questions about this lesson that you want to ask your Bible coach, write them here:

_____

_____

_____

_____

_____

_____

_____

Congratulations on finishing another lesson! You're halfway done! The next lesson is the Good News!

Will you promise to finish it?

☐ Yes   ☐ No

LESSON 3
GOD IS LOVING

LESSON 3
GOD IS LOVING

Today's lesson is the **Good News** we've all been waiting for! But first, let's review! So far in Lessons 1 and 2, we've learned that God is h_____ and j_____. Since God is holy, He can't tolerate our sin. Since God is just, He can't overlook our sin. If this were all we knew about God, we would all be doomed.

But now for the Good News . . . The Bible also teaches another truth about God—"God is love" (1 John 4:8). As we mentioned in the last lesson, God loves us so much that He has provided a way for all sinful people to have a relationship with Him and to live with Him forever. Now *that's* Good News!

JESUS, GOD'S ANSWER TO OUR SIN PROBLEM

John 3:16 is one of the most familiar and loved verses in the Bible, and one of the first verses that children are encouraged to memorize. It tells the Good News of God's love plainly and simply! I encourage you to read it out loud:

> **For God so loved the world, that he gave his only Son, that whoever believes in him should not perish but have eternal life. ~John 3:16**

1. Let's talk about the first part of this verse.

At the very beginning it tells us *why* God wanted to make a way for us to be forgiven: "God so l_____ the world." Remember . . . God is loving!

Then the verse tells us *what* God did because He loved us: "He g_____ his only Son." Do you know who God's Son is? J_____

The next lesson will tell us more about the amazing news found in the second part of this verse. For now, let's pause and talk about Jesus, the Son of God, who is God's answer to our problem of sin.

During the Christmas season, you've probably seen manger scenes with Mary, Joseph, and baby Jesus. God's plan for us was to send Jesus, His perfect Son, to rescue us from our sin.

2. God used an angel to tell Mary and Joseph that Mary would give birth to Jesus.

> **She will bear a son, and you shall call his name Jesus, for he will save his people from their sins. ~Matthew 1:21**

What did the angel tell Mary and Joseph to name their baby? J_____

Why did Jesus come to earth? To save His people f_____ their s_____

Yes! Jesus is the only One who can save us from our sin!

God's Exchange

3. The angel gave Jesus another name that tells us who He is.

> **"Behold, the virgin shall conceive and bear a son, and they shall call his name Immanuel" (which means, God with us). ~Matthew 1:23**

What other name did the angel say would describe Jesus? I_____
This name means that Jesus is "G_____ with us."

Jesus is the Son of God, who is equal with God! (*mind blown*) Jesus left heaven, a perfect place, and came to be born on earth, where everyone is a sinner. He came to earth in a human body so that He could die to take the punishment you deserve! He came to earth to trade places with you.

Jesus Is Our Substitute

You have probably seen many crosses. Sometimes people wear a cross as jewelry. You may have seen three crosses on a hillside. But did you know that those crosses are actually symbols to remind us of how Jesus died? When He was on earth, criminals were sometimes punished by being hung on a cross.

4. Jesus came to earth and lived a perfect life; even though He never sinned, He suffered a terrible death on a cross.

> **But God shows His love for us in that while we were still sinners, Christ died for us [instead of us]. ~Romans 5:8**

Who was the sinner deserving to die?

☐ Me   ☐ Jesus

Who was the One who died?

☐ Me   ☐ Jesus

5. This verse tells us that Jesus took our punishment on Himself when He died on the cross.

> **For Christ also suffered once for sins, the righteous for the unrighteous, that he might bring us to God. ~1 Peter 3:18**

Christ is another name for Jesus.

Who is the righteous person that did not deserve to die?

☐ Me   ☐ Jesus

Who is the unrighteous person that Jesus died for?

☐ Me   ☐ Jesus

That's right; in this verse, Jesus is the *righteous* one and you and I are the *unrighteous* ones. He wants to take your punishment on Himself. Isn't it incredible that a holy, just God would love us *so* much that He would send His perfect Son, Jesus, to die in our place! But there's even more!

Jesus Is Our Righteousness

6. Not only did Jesus take the punishment of death that we deserve for our sin, but He also offers to give us something amazing.

> **For our sake he [God] made him [Jesus] to be sin who knew no sin, so that in him we might become the righteousness of God.
> ~2 Corinthians 5:21**

Jesus took the punishment we earned and offers to give us His

r_____!

To be righteous means to be perfectly right with God. Yes, Jesus offers to make you righteous—acceptable to God!

To better understand this truth, follow the instructions below:

Write your name in the blank on the chart below:

GOD'S EXCHANGE

_____'s Record | Jesus' Record

✓Lying
✓Stealing
✓Cheating
✓Separated From God

✓Holy
✓Just
✓Accepted by God
✓Free to live with God

Now, cross out your name and write "Jesus" above it.

Now, cross out "Jesus" on the right side and write your name above it! (The *Good News* part!)

Do you get it? Jesus wants to change places with you! (*mind blown*) Jesus took *your* sins and wants to give you *His* perfect record! This allows you to have a relationship with a holy, just God and a home in heaven! See, we told you there was Good News in this lesson!

OUR RESCUE

7. Want some more Good News? Jesus did not stay dead!

> **Christ died for our sins . . . he was buried . . . he was raised on the third day in accordance with the Scriptures. ~1 Corinthians 15:3-4**

What happened after Jesus was dead for three days? He w_____
r_____!

This is why Sundays are such special days for Christians. It's the day each week that we celebrate when Jesus rose from the dead! When He rose from the dead, Jesus proved that He was powerful enough to win the victory over sin and its penalty—death in hell! It also proved that God accepted Jesus' payment for our sins.

Yes, God is holy and cannot tolerate sin; He is just and cannot overlook sin. The penalty for our sin is death, but Jesus died in our place. When He rose again, He defeated death and now He can give us new life. God loves you so much that He sent His perfect Son, Jesus, to defeat the penalty of sin for all of us sinners!

If you were to talk to God about what you have learned in this Bible lesson today, what would you tell Him? _____

_____

_____

_____

Lesson 4 will tell you how to accept God's gift of salvation from sin and its penalty. If you don't want to wait to find out, feel free to ask your Bible coach to show you from the Bible how to make the exchange Jesus offers you.

If you have any questions about this lesson that you want to ask your Bible coach, write them here:

_____

_____

_____

_____

_____

_____

_____

Congratulations on finishing another lesson! You're almost done—don't quit now!

Will you promise to finish Lesson 4?

☐ Yes   ☐ No

LESSON 4
GOD IS FULL OF GRACE

LESSON 4

God Is Full of Grace

So far we have seen that God is h_____ and cannot tolerate sin (Lesson 1), that He is j_____ and cannot overlook sin (Lesson 2), and that He is l_____ and cannot ignore our problem (Lesson 3)! God loved us so much, He sent J_____ to earth to live a perfect life and die in our place to pay for our sin. The final truth we will learn in this book is that God is full of grace.

God offers to give us both mercy and grace.

• *Mercy* means that we don't get the punishment we deserve. Here's an illustration that might help you. Let's say that you misbehave at school and deserve a punishment of losing recess time. But your teacher talks to you and says she is going to show you mercy and allow you to still have your recess.

• *Grace* means that you get something you don't deserve. For example, imagine waking up one morning and you are just grumpy. No one wants to be around you. But even though you're not the nicest kid that day, your mom extends grace to you by taking you to get ice cream.

1. God is full of both grace and mercy!

> **But you are a God ready to forgive, gracious and merciful, slow to anger and abounding in steadfast love. ~Nehemiah 9:17**

> **For the wages of sin is death, but the free gift of God is eternal life in Christ Jesus our Lord. ~Romans 6:23**

What punishment do we deserve because of our sin? D_____

Because God is full of mercy, He sent Jesus to take our punishment so that He can forgive our sins.

What gift of God does He offer us instead? E_____ L_____

Because God is full of grace, Jesus not only took our punishment but also offers us the gift of His perfect righteousness!

To picture this, circle "Jesus" on the gift box and write your name on the tag. Jesus is the gift, and with Him comes forgiveness of sins and eternal life in heaven.

Today's lesson will teach you how you can have a relationship with God by receiving the gift of Jesus as your own Lord and Savior.

God's Gift of Jesus

2. Let's go back to John 3:16 and look at the second part of that verse. It tells us how to have everlasting life.

> **For God so loved the world, that he gave his only Son, that whoever believes in him [Jesus] should not perish [die] but have eternal life. ~John 3:16**

What did God give to the world? His only S_____

Why did He give Jesus to us? So that we would not p_____

What does this verse say we have to do to "not perish but have eternal life"?
B_____ in Jesus

3. Here's another verse that tells you how to accept the gift so you can have your sins forgiven.

| **Believe in the Lord Jesus, and you will be saved. ~Acts 16:31**

Once again, the Bible says we need to do what to be saved? B_____ in the L_____ J_____

Most of the time in life, you have to do something to earn valuable things. If you want money, you have to work for it. If you want good grades, you have to study. If you want good friends, you have to spend time with them. People think it's the same way with getting eternal life. They think they have to do a lot of good works or give a lot of money. Let's look at what the Bible says about our good works.

4. List all the things you learn from these verses about how we are saved from the punishment for our sins.

| **For by grace you have been saved through faith. And this is not your own doing; it is the gift of God, not a result of works, so that no one may boast. ~Ephesians 2:8-9**

It's by g_____

Through f_____

Not of y_____ own doing

It is the g_____ of God

Not a result of w_____

When you receive a gift from someone, how much do you have to pay for it?

☐ Nothing   ☐ The amount of money it's worth

When you receive a gift from someone, how much do you have to work to earn it?

☐ **None**   ☐ **The amount of time it's worth**

You see, if something is a gift, it's free! Jesus paid the price, and He wants to give it to you! If you have to work for it or pay for it, it wouldn't be a gift! It's the same with the gift of eternal life. Ephesians 2:8-9 tells us that it is "by grace" (it's undeserved) and it is "through faith" (by believing).

MY FAITH IN JESUS ALONE

Maybe you've been thinking that you have to be good enough to earn eternal life in heaven. This illustration will help you! Here is a picture of two chairs side by side. One chair represents Jesus' finished work for you. Write your name on the other chair.

Imagine sitting in the chair labeled "Your Good Works". Sitting in the chair representing your own good works means that you're putting your trust in what you can do to earn eternal life. What would you have to do to the chair you are sitting in before you could move to the chair labeled "Jesus' Work"?

☐ **Nothing**   ☐ **Get out of the chair representing my good works**

Sitting in the chair labeled "Jesus' Work" means that you're putting your complete faith and trust in the fact that Jesus alone paid the penalty for your sin when He died on the cross, and you can do nothing to earn it. In the same way, you have to *stop* trusting in your own good works and *place your trust in what Jesus has already done* for you on the cross.

What if you wanted the best of both worlds, so you tried to sit in both chairs? Why did you get out of the chair representing your own works? (Because you doubted they were enough to get you to heaven!) Then why aren't you sitting only in the chair representing Jesus' finished work? (You doubt Jesus is enough.) You see, when you try to trust your good works plus Jesus, you're actually showing that you doubt Jesus is enough. So, you have three options:

• **Trust Jesus**   • **Trust yourself**   • **Trust in both**

5. Circle the decision God wants you to make.

You must decide to stop trusting yourself and put your trust in Jesus' finished work.

Repent is another word the Bible uses to describe this decision.

| **But unless you repent, you will all likewise perish. ~Luke 13:3**

The word *repent* means to change your mind. Maybe you have been thinking that your sins are not that bad. You have to change your mind about that. Maybe you've been thinking that you can do enough good works to get into heaven. You have to change your mind about that. To receive God's gift of grace, you have to change your mind about your sin and place your faith in Jesus.

Imagine being in a rowboat on a river with a huge waterfall. The water is moving so fast that it is pulling your boat toward the waterfall, so you turn your boat around and row as hard as you can away from the waterfall. *But* the water is too strong! Even though you are rowing away from the waterfall, the water is still pulling you toward it.

6. Imagine that someone on the shore throws you a rope, and it lands right in your lap. Now you have a choice to make.

What would happen if you grabbed the rope?

☐ **I would be rescued.**   ☐ **I would go over the waterfall.**

What would happen if you kept trying to row instead of grabbing the rope?

☐ **I would be rescued.**   ☐ **I would go over the waterfall.**

If you were in that boat, what would you do?

☐ **I would grab the rope.**   ☐ **I would try to rescue myself.**

That water is like your sin. It is pulling you to destruction. Those oars are like your own good works and religious activities. You may be working very hard, but your good works are not enough to save you. Your sin is too strong. Jesus is like that rope. He is your only hope of salvation from sin and hell. What will you do with Jesus?

Do you believe that you are a sinner?

☐ **Yes**   ☐ **No**

Do you believe that because you are a sinner, you deserve death in hell?

☐ **Yes**   ☐ **No**

Do you believe that Jesus loves you and paid the punishment for your sin when He died on the cross?

☐ **Yes**   ☐ **No**

Are you willing to follow Jesus and put your trust in Him, right now?

☐ **Yes**   ☐ **No**

If your answers were yes, talk to God right now.

Here is a sample prayer, but praying "just the right words" isn't what saves you. Your choice to depend on Jesus alone is what saves you from sin and its penalty. You can use this prayer as a guide, or you can just talk to Him from your heart.

> Dear Jesus, I am a sinner, and you are a holy God. I deserve the punishment of death in hell. I believe that You loved me enough to send Jesus to die in my place. I want to follow You, Jesus. Please forgive my sins and exchange my sinful record for Your perfect one. Give me the gift of eternal life in heaven. Right now, I place my trust in You alone to save me.
> Thank You, Jesus. Amen.

Write down what you told Him.

_____

_____

_____

_____

Did you pray to ask Jesus to forgive you?

☐ Yes   ☐ No

Based on the verses in the Bible that you have read in this lesson, if you were to die right now, where would you go? _____

If you were to die five years from now, where would you go? _____

ENDING THOUGHTS

Remember, it's not about what you feel or even what you think. It's about what God has promised. John 3:16 is a great verse to remind you of God's promise to give eternal life to those who believe. Copy it on the lines below:

> **For God so loved the world, that he gave his only Son, that whoever believes in him should not perish but have eternal life. ~John 3:16**

_____

_____

_____

_____

How long is eternal?

☐ 10 years   ☐ 100 years   ☐ Forever!

How long will you have forgiveness of sins?

☐ **10 years**   ☐ **100 years**   ☐ **Forever!**

If you had died yesterday, or before you made this decision, where would you have gone? _____

If you have any questions about this lesson that you want to ask your Bible coach, write them here:

_____

_____

_____

_____

_____

Congratulations on finishing this Bible study! Good job! Get your Bible coach to help you make a copy of the certificate on the next page and fill in the blanks to show your hard work in finishing this book!

If you made the decision to accept Jesus as your payment for sins, you are now a follower of Christ, also called a *Christian*! Ask your Bible coach about the next steps as a follower of Christ, including baptism, attending church, and learning more about the Bible. Getting to know God is the journey of a lifetime!

Tell everyone you know that you've trusted Jesus. It's the most important decision anyone can make!

You have permission to photocopy the certificate on the next page or go to the following website (exchangemessage.org/certificate) to download it for printing.

CERTIFICATE
OF ACHIEVEMENT

HEREBY CERTIFIES THAT

HAS COMPLETED

Discover God's Exchange
The Gospel for Youth

COMPLETION AWARD

How to Use This Book

- *Discover God's Exchange* works great as a one-on-one study between an individual and a Bible coach.
- This Bible study may also be used in a class setting where each student has their own copy, and the teacher guides them through the material. Here are a few suggested settings you might want to try:
    - Sunday School
    - After-School Bible Study
    - Youth Group
    - Backyard Bible Club
- In addition, this may be used in larger groups if they are working through a Zoom call or other internet connection. In that case, as in a class setting, the teacher may guide them.
- An ESL (English as a Second Language) class is another great place to use *Discover God's Exchange*. The language is simplified to make the concepts easily understood.

Coaching Options

For all the above settings, it may increase the benefit of the learning experience if there are other activities included before and after that will help students learn best in terms of their learning style. Some suggestions are included in the following section.

Discover God's Exchange is a simplified version of *The Exchange Bible Study*. It might be helpful to consult *The Exchange: Leader's Guide*. You can find this at exchangemessage.org/store.

COACHING SUPPLEMENT

Coach's Notes and Ideas

LESSON 1: GOD IS HOLY

1. Discuss and/or show biographies for historical figures such as Abraham Lincoln, George Washington, etc. Ask students if they have read any biographies and discuss the purpose of those books.

2. Have Bibles available for students to use during the lesson. This would be a great time to show the students how to find the different books of the Bible. Explain how to find them in the Table of Contents. Then find the first Scripture reference mentioned in the lesson: 2 Timothy 3:16. Help students who are unfamiliar with Scripture learn how to find the chapter and verse.

3. After the lesson has been completed, give the students a chance to make a poster to keep with the theme: *God Is Holy*. Have poster board or large sheets of paper and various markers so they can each make a poster to take with them. Ask them to tell the group or the coach where they might display the poster they have made.

4. Strongly urge the students to share what they have learned from this lesson. It may be that they can show the poster they have made and simply explain it to their parents or siblings.

Coach's Notes and Ideas

LESSON 2: GOD IS JUST

1. Briefly discuss last week's lesson about *God Is Holy*. Ask the students where they displayed their posters.

2. Talk about classroom rules. Explain why rules are necessary. Make a list of the rules and then a list of the consequences (punishment) if the rules are broken. Discuss if this concept is justice.

3. Look up the following verses in the Bible that discuss justice: Genesis 18:19, 1 Kings 3:28, 2 Samuel 8:15.

4. After completing the lesson, make posters for the theme *God Is Just*. Provide poster board or large sheets of drawing paper as well as a variety of markers that the students can use to create their posters.

5. Ask the students how they plan to explain to their family or a friend that God is just.

Coach's Notes and Ideas

LESSON 3: GOD IS LOVING

1. Review the concepts from Lessons 1 and 2: *God Is Holy* and *God Is Just*. Ask if there are any questions about God's holiness and God's justice.

2. Ask students how they get news—how they find out about things that are happening in their school, their city, and the world. Follow up with: *Have you ever received good news? What was it about? How did you find out?* After giving the students a chance to discuss this briefly, say, "Today we're going to learn about the most important Good News ever."

3. *Let's open our Bibles to John chapter 3 before we begin so that we are ready when it's time to read an important verse.* This is a great opportunity to allow students to find the book of John in their own Bible. If necessary, have them turn to the Table of Contents and look for John to find the page number. Many students will probably be able to locate John without help. Provide assistance as needed.

4. Provide materials for the students to create a poster for the theme *God Is Loving*. Give them some guidance and show them the materials available for them to use. When they are finished, give them a few minutes to share their work with the other students or with you.

5. Follow up with asking about their plan to show their poster to their family or a friend and asking where they might hang it in their home.

Coach's Notes and Ideas

LESSON 4: GOD IS FULL OF GRACE

1. As you begin today's lesson, start with a short review of the previous three lessons. Getting the students to explain the truths from the previous lessons in their own words will help them to cement it in their minds and souls. (Of course, if they are not correct in what they say, you will need to guide them to the correct understanding.)

2. Ask students to share if they have ever experienced grace. This will be explained in the lesson, but it can help to make them aware and receptive if you discuss it before you begin. If no one has anything to offer, give an example from your own life. Explain that this is what they will be studying so they can look for the answer as they go through the lesson.

3. Ask the students to look up the first verse in their Bibles and keep it open to that spot as you begin the lesson. This is a great opportunity for you to assist students who may not be familiar with finding Scripture references. If you have a student who is struggling to find the verses, you may want to partner them with another student to help them as you go through the lesson.

4. When you have finished the lesson, provide materials for the students to create their final poster using the theme *God Is Full of Grace*. Show them the materials available and let them work on their posters. When they are finished, give them a few minutes to share their work with the other students.

5. Explain that this is the last lesson and the last poster. Ask students if they have kept the previous three posters hanging in a special place at home. Encourage them to hang this last poster with the previous ones after sharing it with their family or a friend. Remind them that these posters can be a daily encouragement to them as they go through each day.